Facts About the Caterpillar

By Lisa Strattin

© 2019 Lisa Strattin

FREE BOOK

FREE FOR ALL SUBSCRIBERS

LisaStrattin.com/Subscribe-Here

BOX SET

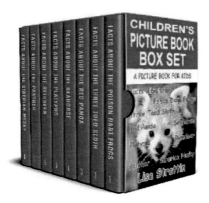

- **FACTS ABOUT THE POISON DART FROGS**
- **FACTS ABOUT THE THREE TOED SLOTH**
- **FACTS ABOUT THE RED PANDA**
- **FACTS ABOUT THE SEAHORSE**
- **FACTS ABOUT THE PLATYPUS**
- **FACTS ABOUT THE REINDEER**
- **FACTS ABOUT THE PANTHER**
- **FACTS ABOUT THE SIBERIAN HUSKY**

LisaStrattin.com/BookBundle

Facts for Kids Picture Books by Lisa Strattin

Little Blue Penguin, Vol 92

Chipmunk, Vol 5

Frilled Lizard, Vol 39

Blue and Gold Macaw, Vol 13

Poison Dart Frogs, Vol 50

Blue Tarantula, Vol 115

African Elephants, Vol 8

Amur Leopard, Vol 89

Sabre Tooth Tiger, Vol 167

Baboon, Vol 174

Sign Up for New Release Emails Here

LisaStrattin.com/subscribe-here

COVER IMAGE

https://www.flickr.com/photos/14583963@N00/10741145185/

ADDITIONAL IMAGES

https://www.flickr.com/photos/dhaskovec/563829051/

https://www.flickr.com/photos/dirk_olbertz/3807136705/

https://www.flickr.com/photos/eurleif/44828147/

https://www.flickr.com/photos/gcwest/6392327991/

https://www.flickr.com/photos/mattx27/5506673037/

https://www.flickr.com/photos/sk8geek/4872777157/

https://www.flickr.com/photos/jonnyrose/6326589885/

https://www.flickr.com/photos/peterkaminski/2508411999/

https://www.flickr.com/photos/agavegirl13/7619412416/

https://www.flickr.com/photos/mreillyphoto/20202568163/

Contents

INTRODUCTION

There are more than 20,000 different species of known caterpillar found all around the world and researchers believe that there are many more that remain undiscovered as new species of butterflies and moths are regularly found in regions where there are few people.

CHARACTERISTICS

The moth caterpillar is well known for being a pest, especially in the fabric industry. One species of caterpillar has destroyed a lot of silk in the far east. This species is known in China as the silkworm.

Generally, most species of caterpillar are considered to be agricultural pests because they can eat their way through large fields of crops, often leaving damage which results in unhealthy or inedible plants, and financial losses for farmers.

Some species are also very poisonous, particularly those species that live in tropical rain forests. Others are only dangerous as caterpillars, meaning when they turn into a moth or butterfly, they no longer have venom.

APPEARANCE

Caterpillars difference in size, color and appearance depending on the species. Some are very brightly colored where others species are quite dull-looking in comparison. Some caterpillars are very hairy, but others are very smooth.

The goal of the appearance of the caterpillar is to intimidate and to keep predators from eating it.

LIFE STAGES

The caterpillar is the baby of both a butterfly and a moth. After around 2-3 weeks, the caterpillar builds itself into a cocoon where it remains for another 2 weeks. The caterpillar then emerges having grown wings – becoming a butterfly or moth.

LIFE SPAN

The caterpillar only lives for about 3 to 4 weeks, then it becomes a butterfly or a moth.

SIZE

Generally, caterpillars are 1 to 2 inches long.

HABITAT

Caterpillars live all over the world. They are found mostly in quiet pastures, they particularly like fields of crops and grassy areas where there are lots of leaves to eat.

DIET

In most cases, the caterpillar, like the butterfly, is herbivorous but the diets of the caterpillar and the butterfly are very different. Butterflies use their long straw-like tongues to drink the nectar out of flowers, which is a change that occurs in the process where the caterpillar becomes a butterfly. Caterpillars mainly feed on leaves, plants and flowering plants and big holes can often be found in leaves indicating the presence of a caterpillar.

There are a number of species of caterpillar known to be carnivorous and eat a variety of insects that pass them. One caterpillar species found in Hawaii, hooks itself onto a leaf where it stands very straight trying to catch passing bugs.

ENEMIES

Due to their small size and worm-like shape, caterpillars are preyed upon by many different species of animal. The main predators of the caterpillar are birds and large insects like wasps. They are also commonly eaten by small mammals and reptiles.

SUITABILITY AS PETS

You could keep a caterpillar as a pet, but only for a little while. Since it is only a caterpillar for a few weeks, it would build the cocoon and emerge as a butterfly or moth. This activity, keeping a caterpillar and watching it change, is sometimes referred to as a "Butterfly Birthday" and is something that many elementary classrooms experience as a class project.

COLOR ME

COLOR ME

COLOR ME

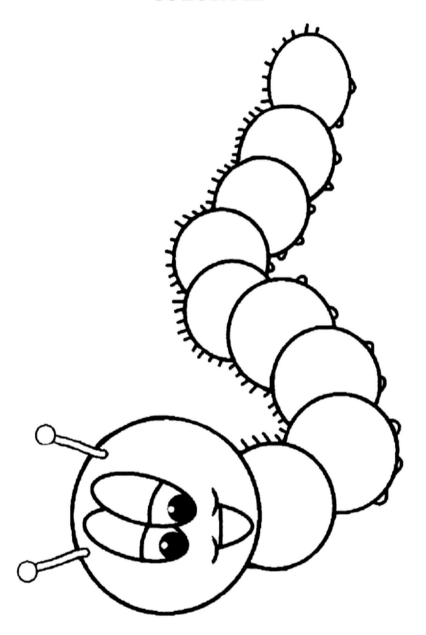

COLOR ME

COLOR ME

COLOR ME

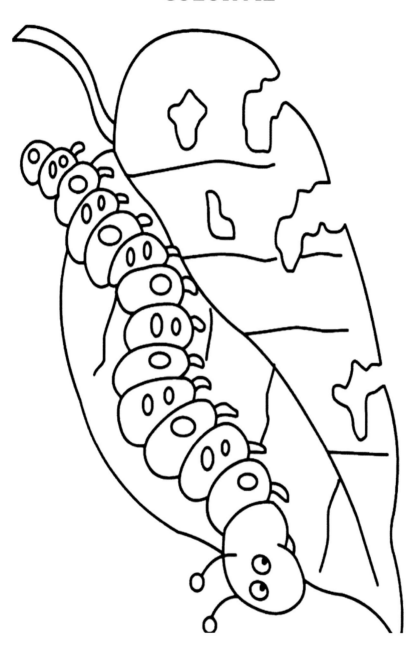

COLOR ME

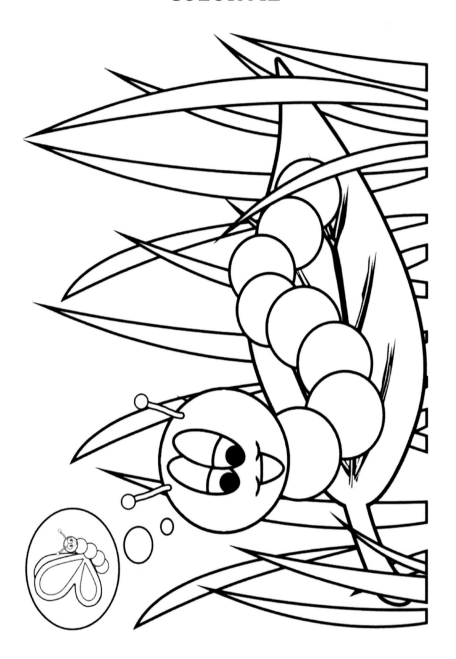

COLOR ME

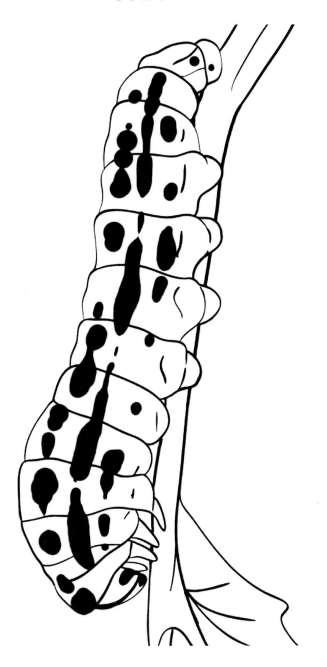

COLOR ME

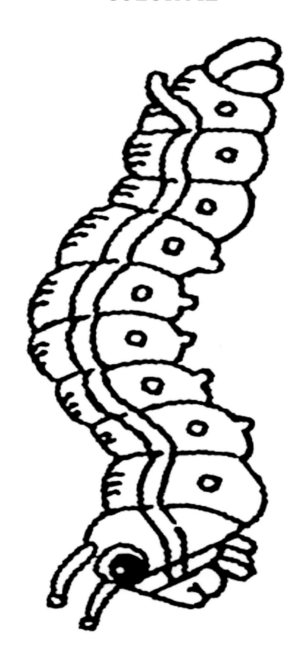

Please leave me a review here:

LisaStrattin.com/Review-Vol-242

For more Kindle Downloads Visit Lisa Strattin Author Page on Amazon Author Central

amazon.com/author/lisastrattin

To see upcoming titles, visit my website at LisaStrattin.com– most books available on Kindle!

LisaStrattin.com

FREE BOOK

FOR ALL SUBSCRIBERS – SIGN UP NOW

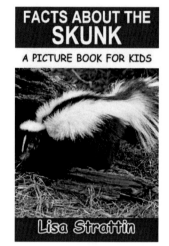

LisaStrattin.com/Subscribe-Here

LisaStrattin.com/Facebook

LisaStrattin.com/Youtube

Made in United States
North Haven, CT
21 September 2024

57736665R00024